Tell Them I Love Them

A Letter To Prisoners

by
Diann Emerson

Published by Ethereal Wings Publishing
PO Box 948
Locust Grove, VA 22508

Scripture taken from the New King James Version®.
Copyright © 1982 by Thomas Nelson.
Used by permission.

ISBN: 978-0-578-35836-9

This book is a memoir. It reflects the author's present
recollections of experiences over time. Names have
been changed, some events have been compressed,
and some dialogue has been recreated.

Table of Contents

To you, with love.

I pray that you "may be able to comprehend with all the saints what is the width and length and depth and height – to know the love of Christ which passes knowledge; that you may be filled with all the fullness of God."

~ Ephesians 3:18,19

God doesn't love me. I've had so many bad things happen. Where was he in the hurt? He threw me into the rejected pile, but somehow, I lived. I reject him because he rejects me.

God doesn't want to help me. I've failed too many times and I'll never measure up. I take care of myself because who wants to help a prisoner? No one, or I wouldn't be locked up.

God lives somewhere called heaven while I can barely get by. Life won't get better for me because I can't seem to get ahead. I have no hope.

If this is how you feel, if any part of this is true for you, please keep reading.

Chapter 1

AWAKENED

I sat numbly on the edge of my bed. Not my oldest son. This must be a mistake! He came home last night. He was standing near the front door with his palms at his thighs. His eyes were clear and handsome. His brother stared at him.

"How was work?" I asked.

"Long day. But two people wanted more info."

"That's good! Maybe they'll decide it's time to replace their windows. Feel free to use my sunscreen next time."

"Who needs sunscreen?"

"I know you're up to something," said his brother.

"I'm not up to anything." His jaw tightened.

His sister looked in his eyes.

"Are you okay?"

"I'm fine."

"He's probably just tired and hungry. Do you want some pizza?" I said. The spicy smell of pepperoni rose from the box.

He sat on the loveseat with two slices and a soda, watching TV with his dad when he wasn't texting. The Lions were defeating the Bears in a prerecorded game.

I felt relieved that he was making the right decision. We had given him a week to get help for substance abuse or move out. If he had to pay for his own living expenses, he would have less money to buy drugs. I headed for the shower.

His dad came to get ready for bed.

"Do you think he's staying?" I said.

"I don't know. He went for a walk."

"At eleven? Did he say why?"

"He said he just wanted to go for a walk."

Performing my nightly check, I left the door unlocked, hoping he would be back by midnight. He had to be—or sleep somewhere else. That was the rule.

Still wrestling with my pillow and blankets at 3:00 a.m., I went searching for him. His bed was cold and his parking spot was empty. I locked the door.

Chapter 2

THE TRUTH

The phone rang at approximately 6:15 a.m.

"May I speak to Diann Emerson?"

"This is Diann."

"I'm an officer with the regional jail. I'm calling to let you know we have your son in custody," he said.

"Thank you for letting me know."

"You're welcome. Have a nice day."

"Wait. What's he being held for? A drug charge or a DUI?"

"First-degree murder, ma'am."

My world stopped. "What did you say?"

"First-degree murder, ma'am. I'm sorry."

He hung up. For a moment, I couldn't feel anything. And then, I felt everything.

The public information officer contacted me later that morning.

"Hello, Mrs. Emerson. I'm calling to ensure you've been informed of your son's arrest before the local newspaper publishes the story."

"An officer from the regional jail called this morning to let me know. Is it possible someone else was driving my son's car and they have the wrong person in custody?"

"I'm not at liberty to give you that information. Because he's twenty, he's considered an adult, by law. I can say he is our only suspect."

"I see."

"Community services are available if you need support. Let us know if you have any other questions."

"Thank you."

I appreciated the offer I had no intention of taking. They didn't understand. What I needed was the truth. He called five days later.

"Mom, it's me."

"Is it true?"

"Yes, it is."

"Why?"

"Because my life wasn't going anywhere."

"So you took another man's life? Only God can help you now."

I handed the phone to his dad.

Chapter 3

EYES OPEN

I struggled to get to church the following Sunday. I felt lost walking through the familiar parking lot. A woman approached. Her hug anchored me.

We had been members of the same church for five years. Sometimes I would say good morning or thank you as she offered me grape juice and a wafer for communion. That was about it.

I remembered when her sons were arrested and she was crying. Other members supported her family, but not me. I didn't understand what the big deal was. *Guess they're not perfect after all. They'll have to pay back their debt to society.* Yet, God sent her to comfort me.

"How are you?" she asked.

"This is a nightmare I wish I could wake up from," I said.

"I understand." She nodded as tears welled in her eyes.

"I almost walked away from God because I couldn't understand why He didn't stop our sons. Now, I know; He gave them free will. How's your son doing?"

"I don't know. We haven't talked much."

"Are you helping him?"

"I helped him before he committed a crime. He chose his path, and now he can live with it."

"Our sons were only seventeen and fifteen," she said. "We didn't know they were a part of a theft ring until the police came. We wrote to them every day and visited them every week. We always accepted their calls and they were so thankful. They said some prisoners didn't have any visitors. There was no mail coming for them. They had no one to call because no one cared."

"Your boys are blessed to have you," I said.

"Did you know you can put money into an account for your son?"

"No, I haven't dealt with this before."

"He can use it to buy food, toiletries, clothes, and stamps."

"I thought our tax dollars paid for that."

"They get some food and clothing, but it's not enough. Our sons would have gone to bed hungry if we didn't help them."

"I didn't know that."

"You really should help your son, as much as you can. He needs you now more than ever. You're hurting, but don't stop loving him. Jesus does that for us. If there's anything we can do, let us know." She hugged me. We went in for service.

My husband and children were waiting for me. I wasn't sure how people would react when they heard the news. I expected some would turn their backs on us. Instead, they encouraged us and mourned with us. For the first time, people shared their family's experience of incarceration with me. Like us, it affected them when one of their own was taken away in cuffs.

The senior pastor of another church came to pray. He read the story and knew where God wanted him. His congregation planned to walk the same route my son took the night of his arrest. They wanted to give hope and hot chocolate on Christmas Eve to people they met along the way.

They gave me strength I didn't have. Every prayer lifted me out of darkness when I couldn't see light. I never imagined the outpouring of love we experienced that day and in the months to come. Our family in Jesus was bigger than I realized.

Chapter 4

WHERE DID MOMMA GO WRONG?

It made the front page of the newspaper and we weren't subscribers, but we got that edition. HOMICIDE IS CITY'S FIRST SINCE APRIL 2009. A large picture of police, yellow tape, and a bloodstained driveway. A small picture of my son's face, someone I thought I knew. I wanted to throw it away, but a friend urged me to keep it.

"You'll need proof it really happened," she predicted.

We checked the internet hourly for details.

Homicide rattles city.

Suspect charged.

Argument over illegal narcotics.

Stabbing death.

Incarcerated without bond.

Stories of crime and arrest were no longer just sad articles in the news; they were flesh and blood, life and death. Several comments followed the news releases, but one wouldn't let go of me.

"Where did Momma go wrong?"

Well-meaning people insisted it wasn't my fault. Some thought I should snap out of it because there were others who needed me. All I knew was, I couldn't run from it anymore. I locked myself in my bedroom and refused to see anyone, not even the pastor.

I slumped into my bed and came face-to-face with the truth. My son's hand drove a K-bar through another man's heart, but my hand was the first to hold his.

I met his biological father in the lobby of a Marine Corps barracks. He was on duty, and I was returning from a trip home to my grandparents' house.

"My name is Corporal DeMay and I'm waiting for my luggage. The airline said they'll deliver it by eleven p.m. tonight."

"I can bring it to you when it gets here. What's your room number?"

"Room 408."

He knocked on the door a little before eleven.

"Here's your luggage. Where would you like it?"

"I'll take it. Thanks."

"You're welcome. My name is Sean, by the way. I work on the flight line. How about you?"

"I'm with the training department."

"Do you like it?"

"It's all right, but I don't like Yuma. I'm trying to get out of here and they keep denying my request."

"I know what you mean, it's hot and boring. You're probably tired after traveling all day. Would you like to talk over dinner sometime?"

I took a closer look…he was cute.

"Yeah, that sounds good."

"Are you busy on Thursday around seven?"

"I don't think so."

"Will I see you then?"

"Okay, see you on Thursday."

That date led to more dates, and I fell hard. He told me he loved me and we would get married. He had two daughters from a previous marriage, and I thought he wouldn't leave if I was the mother of his firstborn son.

Using the rhythm method to track my monthly cycle, I invited him over on the days I was most likely to conceive. I didn't ask him if he was ready, nor consider the life that child could have. I only thought of myself.

At twelve weeks pregnant, I called to tell him I heard a heartbeat. Tears flowed, wishing he had been there to share that moment. I desperately wanted a loving family with him, but broken promises don't build a future together. He left for West Virginia in his red pickup with a bed full of stuff and a dishonorable discharge.

He was gone, and so was my desire to live. I wasn't close to God, but He was close to me. His presence saved me when no one else could.

Staff told me that life as I knew it would be over if I kept the baby. My grandfather wanted to disown me and burn anything I left at the house. Not knowing what to do, I asked Corporal T, who was like a brother.

"What should I do?"

"I can't make that decision for you."

"Okay, what would you do if it were you, then?"

"Where I come from, abortion ain't cool, Shawty."

I moved out of the barracks and into a studio apartment on the third floor. My mom came to help me for three weeks. After thirty-one hours of labor, my beautiful son was born.

Six months later, on the earliest date they could send me, I got orders to the Noncommissioned Officer School. The Corps didn't look favorably on single parents, and I had to excel to reenlist. I started a vegan diet to meet weight restrictions and to fit into my uniforms, because I couldn't afford new ones. I ran more than I had to, lifted weights, and took high-intensity aerobics classes.

I expected the physical training (PT) to be demanding. What I didn't know was the staff sergeant leading PT was exceptionally fit, even by Corps standards.

After a vigorous warmup and nine-mile run through the orange groves, hydration seemed impossible. I steadied myself against a tree. I gave my all to finish well and was more than ready for the air-conditioned classroom.

"Line up now for pyramid pull-ups," he yelled. Followed by wind sprints across the field and more exercises.

I was twenty-one, but by evening, I shuffled like I was ninety-one. I fed my son, bathed him, and put him to bed. He cried, I ironed and studied, and the neighbors came regularly to see if everything was all right.

PT got easier for me. Leaving my son with babysitters never did.

I reenlisted in a career that would support us so we wouldn't have to depend on others. My grandparents cared for him while I completed Air Traffic Control School in Memphis. They grew to love him as the son they didn't have.

I married the Marine who sat next to me thirty days after meeting him. We graduated and drove to an air station in California—my son, his new dad, me, and his unborn brother. We faced many challenges that were too big for us, but not for God.

Yes, I take the blame for not giving my son the loving, nurturing childhood he needed and deserved. I didn't give him a good foundation to grow on. What I gave him was impatience, anger, selfishness, and a war zone. I tried to change myself, but I couldn't. Sick of feeling like a failure every night my head hit the pillow, I cried out.

"Lord, I don't want to put my hands on him in anger anymore. Use my hands for love."

I changed slowly. The hands that once harmed him now protected him. Yes, I could have done a better job. But I'm thankful for the good I wouldn't have had apart from God.

I sat up in bed and looked around my room and at my life. There was nothing I could give the victim's family to compensate for their loss. I couldn't bring him back to his mother's arms. His heart would not beat again.

"Dear Lord, forgive me for the pain and suffering I've caused. Heal what I have broken. Be strong where I am weak.

"As much as I can do time with my son, let me do it. I want to be there when he walks through the release door and transitions to life on the outside. I want to give him home-cooked meals and a comfortable bed. Show him vast, open places. No. More. Bars."

Chapter 5

A Choice

It was tempting to look at the past and believe the future wouldn't be any brighter; like the good news of the Bible was true for everyone except me and my family. Bad things happened to us, and there was nothing I could do about it. I thought about giving up and giving in to hopelessness. Then God showed me the truth.

"I have set before you life and death, blessing and cursing; therefore choose life, that both you and your descendants may live" (Deut. 30:19). God gives us all a choice that no one and nothing can take away.

As a friend shared with me, it's like having money in your hand.

"What will you do with it? How will you spend your life?" she asked.

I had a choice. I could believe God and choose life, or I could do it my way and choose death.

Not believing His Word meant doing things the way I had always done them, and that wasn't working for me.

Believe God. It was easier to read those words than to live by them. I had to believe that He is God and He is good. He's not holding out on me and I won't miss out if I do things His way. It was hard to trust Him because I was looking at Him as a person and not as a heavenly Father who has never hurt me. I had to take it to Him.

"Oh, God, things continue to get worse. I desperately need You. Yes, I want beauty for ashes."

"If you ask anything in My name, I will do it. If you love Me, keep My commandments" (John 14:14,15).

"I know, I ask in Your name. But I don't think it'll change anything. How are You going to help us?"

"'For My thoughts are not your thoughts, Nor are your ways My ways,'" says the LORD" (Isa. 55:8). "Walk by faith, not by sight" (2 Cor. 5:7).

"I'm coming before Your throne, asking for Your mercy and Your grace. Will You help us?"

"'Do not be afraid; only believe'" (Mark 5:36).

He would give us beauty for ashes (Isa. 61:3).

I was getting things done at home and putting money on my son's books, but it didn't seem to be enough. And if tragedy happened to us, it could happen to anyone. People were dying without knowing Jesus as their Lord and Savior. I couldn't forget that.

One Sunday morning, *Between A Rock And A Grace Place,* a book by Carol Kent, was waiting for me at church. A friend thought the author's experience would help me. Carol's only son, Jason Kent, was sentenced to life without parole for murder. For weeks I refused to read it. I couldn't bear the thought of her son receiving a life sentence for the same crime mine committed. I couldn't accept that he would live the rest of his life behind bars.

She included letters from Jason. In one letter, he described the state-issued footwear and trousers inmates wear when they don't have anyone to deposit money in their account. He shared the hardship of wearing the wrong size shoes and trousers, and what they have to do to repair them. He wrote, "These little things take away part of our dignity—and if we let these common practices get to us, it produces discontent." Jason's words shot straight into my chest.

Inmates are genuine people with actual needs. They are not numbers hidden behind walls to be forgotten. They made mistakes, just like me. Some served time knowing they were innocent.

Who walks with them and comforts them? Does anyone encourage them and give them hope? Will someone share Jesus with them before they eat their last meal? Do they know they are loved?

How could I be so ignorant and selfish? God wasn't joking when the Word said, "Remember the prisoners as if chained with them—those who are mistreated—since you yourselves are in the body also" (Heb. 13:3). And, "For there is not a just man on earth who does good And does not sin" (Eccles. 7:20). Why did I ever think I was better because I hadn't been incarcerated? I repented and asked for forgiveness. His love flooded my heart like a tidal wave and then . . . I looked up.

"Is this from You, God? Are you sure? They're going to think I'm like Betty Crocker, and what's Betty Crocker going to do for them? Bake them some cookies? I feel so inadequate."

If a note dropped from heaven, I would have questioned who wrote it. I prayed for confirmation I could not deny.

Chapter 6

BIG OL' YES

My daughter accidentally arrived at Chick-Fil-A an hour earlier than scheduled. A customer came to her table while she waited. She was a strong, uplifting, and well-dressed Christian in her sixties. She'd suffered the loss of a brother and best friend in the same week. A drug-related shooting took her father from her. She and my daughter shared an understanding only people who have experienced a similar trauma can share.

After catching up, the woman asked, "How's your mother?"

My daughter couldn't remember telling the woman anything about me.

"She's doing good. But she doesn't know what God wants her to do—take more Latin classes or volunteer in prison ministry."

"So, let me get this straight. She doesn't know if God wants her in prison ministry or if He wants her to sit in a foreign language class while people go to hell? Look, people care about themselves. They think about their jobs, their home, their spouse, and what they like to do. When someone has a desire to bring the unpopular gospel of Jesus Christ to inmates, that's from God. What does Jesus have to do? Slap her upside the head with a big ol' yes? Oh, I'll be praying for her."

An hour later, I was at home searching for programs to help my son. I found videos of inmates worshiping God and experiencing spiritual freedom behind bars. I heard testimonies of Christians who minister to them, even those sentenced to death; people united in God's love and grace. A blubbering mess, I prayed again. "Lord, is this where You want me?" My hands shook as I submitted a volunteer request.

That night, my daughter shared her day at work. I knew it was the confirmation I longed for.

Chapter 7

TRAINING

The volunteer organization accepted my request and I enrolled in training. I learned about prison culture, mentoring, and bringing hope. I completed the training. But God had more.

Images of evil flashed on the screen during a Bible study about truth. Wars, suffering, famous trials, and Jeffrey Dahmer. He was on the stand and he looked sincere. Did I see love in his eyes? It made no sense, and I wasn't about to ask the study leaders to rewind.

A quick internet search showed articles of his confession to being a born-again Christian. Is that possible? I pushed it out of my mind. It didn't seem right to think about it for too long. The evil that attacked him might attack me.

Months later, the thoughts returned. They were there when I got ready for bed, ate lunch, and vacuumed. And one day, in a grocery store parking lot, I couldn't take it anymore.

"Lord God, I need Your help. Take these thoughts out of my mind or tell me what You want me to do with them."

I went back to the internet. Wikipedia revealed that Minister Roy Ratcliff, who baptized Jeffrey, had also written a book about his experience. I read *Dark Journey Deep Grace: Jeffrey Dahmer's Story of Faith*.

He writes, "When he was ready, I placed my hands on his head and one shoulder. I said, 'Jeff, upon your confession of faith in Jesus as the Christ, the Son of God, I now baptize you in the name of the Father and of the Son and of the Holy Spirit for the forgiveness of your sins.' I pushed him under the water until he was completely immersed. When his head broke the surface, I said something I always say when I baptize someone. 'Welcome to the family of God!'"

Jesus said, "'And you shall know the truth, and the truth shall make you free'" (John 8:32). Jeffrey Dahmer and I had nothing in common; I was a good citizen. I hadn't murdered, mutilated, or cannibalized people. As a single woman, I'd had affairs with married men, but no one died because of it. I had stolen, lied, and hurt people who hurt me. Okay, my list of sins was pretty long. But his was longer.

God reminded me of His Word. "For there is no difference; for all have sinned and fall short of the glory of God" (Rom. 3:22,23). When measured against a perfect God, no one measures up. We both sinned, and we both needed Jesus.

"For the wages of sin is death, but the gift of God is eternal life in Christ Jesus our Lord" (Rom. 6:23). Blood had to spill. Our sins nailed Jesus to a Roman cross. He took the death penalty for us, giving His life so we could live an abundant life in Him.

Considering eternity, Jeff and I were the same— unable to save ourselves. Without Jesus, we would live our eternal lives in hell. We couldn't earn it; the price was too high. God freely gave it to us in love.

———∞∞∞———

Here is a trustworthy saying that deserves full acceptance: Christ Jesus came into the world to save sinners—of whom I am the worst. But for that very reason I was shown mercy so that in me, the worst of sinners, Christ Jesus might display his un-limited patience as an example for those who would believe in Him and receive eternal life. 1 Timothy 1:15–16 NIV, READ BY JEFFREY DAHMER IN HIS STATEMENT TO THE COURT, 1992 (*Dark Journey Deep Grace*)

Chapter 8

OBSTACLES

"I'm officially a prison ministry volunteer," I said.

"You're too soft," said my pastor.

"But God isn't."

"I know that's right."

A week after online training, I emailed the volunteer coordinator.

"I was wondering if I need to complete more training? I'm not sure what the next step is."

"Your training is complete," she replied. "Your next step is to meet the regional director. He will contact you to meet and discuss placement."

A month later, a new director called me. He apologized for the delay and asked for information to update my file. Coordinating volunteers with opportunities wasn't easy. He would get back to me.

I waited two months and called again. He apologized again for the delay. He was still working on organizing and placement.

Finally, he introduced me to Reverend Dr. Abigail Barnett, a lovely woman with twenty-five years of experience in prison ministry. I could accompany her to a women's prison if I was approved by the DOC. I submitted an application. Denied because I visited my son within twelve months of applying. I prayed.

"God, I know You told me to go. How can I if they won't let me? This feels like a death in my family."

Abigail called a few days later.

"I've been praying about your situation," she said.

"I appreciate your prayers."

"Oh, anytime. I also volunteer at a local jail maintained by the county. You would have to apply again, and it's about an hour-and-a-half drive. Or you could look for something closer."

"Thank you so much. You're one of the few people who haven't tried to talk me out of this. Yeah, I think I'll look for something closer."

I found re-entry programs, but I believed the Lord was asking me to go behind the bars. He wanted me to meet them where they were, to see them, not their crime.

After calling a few more places and not find-
ing what I was looking for, I prayed for wisdom. I
could volunteer at a jail an hour and a half away or
continue to look for a local opportunity. I thought
about Jesus coming all the way from heaven to be
with us. Distance wasn't an issue anymore.

Chapter 9

FORGIVENESS

We approached the gothic building where judges make decisions that affect many lives. Extra police officers patrolled the area. It was cloudy as we entered through the side door.

Our family, friends, and strangers watched as my son came into the courtroom. It was the first time I had seen him in person since his arrest. He was wearing an orange jumper, handcuffed and shackled. I longed to be by his side, even if it meant I would be shackled and cuffed, but the court wouldn't allow it.

It seemed like hours while they poured out evidence against him. I testified about our family life, no longer pretending everything was okay. Now the community knew, and there was nothing to hide. "It is what it is" was a popular saying and it became a favorite of mine.

The judge sentenced him to 40 years with 10 suspended. Our lives were intertwined for twenty years and now he was going where Momma couldn't go.

His brother and sister left the courtroom crying and waited outside. My daughter saw the victim's family and felt like someone pushed her towards them. No one was behind her. She introduced herself.

"My mom wanted you to know how sorry she is. We all wish none of this had ever happened. We should have done more to stop him," she said.

His mother hugged her small frame.

"Baby, we've already forgiven your family. Take care of your mother. She's going to need it."

Do you believe you have done too many bad things for God to forgive you? Do you think, "You don't know what I've done; I have nightmares about my past, and God doesn't want someone like me"?

God knew what you would do during your life-time when He sacrificed His perfect Son to save you.

"For scarcely for a righteous man will one die; yet perhaps for a good man someone would even dare to die. But God demonstrates His own love toward us, in that while we were still sinners, Christ died for us" (Rom. 5:7,8).

Let's look at Jesus's last hours before He died.

"There were also two others, criminals, led with Him to be put to death. And when they had come to the place called Calvary, there they crucified Him, and the criminals, one on the right hand and the other on the left. Then Jesus said, 'Father, forgive them, for they do not know what they do.' And they divided His garments and cast lots. And the people stood looking on. But even the rulers with them sneered, saying, 'He saved others; let Him save Himself if He is the Christ, the chosen of God.' The soldiers also mocked Him, coming and offering Him sour wine, and saying, 'If You are the King of the Jews, save Yourself.' And an inscription also was written over Him in letters of Greek, Latin, and Hebrew: THIS IS THE KING OF THE JEWS. Then one of the criminals who were hanged blasphemed Him, saying, 'If You are the Christ, save Yourself and us.' But the other, answering, rebuked him, saying, 'Do you not even fear God, seeing you are under the same condemnation? And we indeed justly, for we receive the due reward of our deeds; but this Man has done nothing wrong.' Then he said to Jesus, 'Lord, remember me when You come into Your kingdom.' And Jesus said to him, 'Assuredly, I say to you, today you will be with Me in Paradise.' Now it was about the sixth hour, and there was darkness over all the earth until the ninth hour. Then the sun was darkened, and the veil of the temple was torn in two. And when Jesus had cried out with a loud voice, He said, 'Father, into Your hands I commit My spirit.' Having said this, He breathed His last" (Luke 23:32–46).

Questions to consider:

Who was led with Jesus to be put to death?

What did Jesus ask His Father to do for them?

What did Jesus say to the man who believed when he asked Him to remember him?

Did his sins keep him from salvation?

Neither have you committed too many sins to be saved.

The gospels of Matthew, Mark, Luke, and John are written from four different perspectives to more fully understand the life Jesus lived on earth, His death, and His resurrection. The book of John is a good place to start.

Chapter 10

UNCONDITIONALLY

True love is loyal at all times; it is patient and kind. It seeks the best for you. It doesn't get mad easily and doesn't keep a list of what you've done wrong. Love doesn't have joy in injustice, but rejoices in the truth. "Love never fails" (1 Cor. 13:8).

Maybe you've given up searching for love or doubt it's even real. You've felt the crushing weight of tragedy. It's a fight just to stay alive. The pain comes back after the high wears off, the punch of rejection still hurts, and the face of the abuser won't leave. The wrong path looked like the right one—and where did everyone go who promised to walk it with you?

I would like to share excerpts of a letter from my son and my response to him.

Dear Mom,

I've been meaning to write to you, but not under these circumstances. As you already know, I'm in segregation again. Mom, I am so sorry I ended up here. Period. It's like every time I have something good going for me, I screw it up.

When the officer brought me back to the cell, I was finally alone. Alone, in my own prison, nothing to distract from thoughts building for several months. All the anger, sadness, regret, hatred forced below the surface. Can't allow anyone to see it, always running from it, pretending everything is okay. Focused on being a gangster and keeping composure.

Truth be told, I'd trade it all in to be a good son that went to college or joined the military and made my family proud. I could have been a successful, married man. I threw my whole life away with no consideration of the consequences. No thought of anyone else, not thinking about the people that care.

I am a failure at life. And I am so sorry, Mom. Every day the guilt is overwhelming and just beneath the surface. Back here, I can't run from the memories or the pain. Forced to deal with it all and feeling no self-worth, I wondered if this is how you felt before you found God. I begged for His forgiveness, again. No matter how hard I try to do things my way, the outcome is always the same. It's insanity.

I go for my hearing on Monday, the 24th. Please wait for the verdict before deciding whether to disown me. I really care about the family and I'm trying hard to behave. Please don't hate me. I don't know why I do what I do. Please pray for me.

Love, Your Son

Dear Son,

Thank you for writing to me. I'm always excited to get your letters. The fact that you're in segregation does not diminish my love for you. Whatever the outcome of the hearing, I love you!

My love for you is not based on what you do or don't do. You don't have to earn it or prove anything to me. You are not a failure. No matter what, you are my son and I love you. I want you to stay out of trouble because I don't want you or someone else to get hurt.

As I read your letter, I learned something about God I knew with my mind, but not with my heart. It hurts Him when we sin because it distances us from Him. Not because He walked away, but because we did. When we come back and ask for forgiveness, He forgives us because He wants to. Nothing can separate us from His love. Your words made me realize, even if you were the president of the United States, it would not change the way I feel about you. How much more does God feel about us?

You said you're trying hard to behave and you love us. I believe you. You're an important part of the family and we love you too! No one can take your place. I pray you feel God's love surrounding you and in your heart. Don't give up. We have hope in Him!

I miss you.

Love, Mom

Chapter 11

As You Are

When I visit my son, and I'm blessed to be there during count, I want to stand with him. I want to answer with his name and our address when the officer asks for his number and pod. Incarceration doesn't change who he is or where he belongs.

God wants you to be His child. He made you in His image (Gen. 1:27). You were like Him when you comforted someone or encouraged them when they wanted to give up. When you shared your soup or coffee knowing they couldn't pay it back. When you protected people who couldn't defend themselves, they needed you and you were there. You felt what He feels when you stood for a cause you believe in because He stood for you.

You were right when you looked at the walls and realized there's more to life than this.

Jesus says, "I have come that they may have life, and that they may have it more abundantly" (John 10:10).

"For I know the thoughts that I think toward you, says the LORD, thoughts of peace and not of evil, to give you a future and a hope" (Jer. 29:11).

The choices you made or what others say about you cannot change your value to God. What are you worth to God? The life of His own beloved Son. You are priceless. I want to say that again. You are priceless.

"For God so loved the world that He gave His only begotten Son, that whoever believes in Him should not perish but have everlasting life. For God did not send His Son into the world to condemn the world, but that the world through Him might be saved" (John 3:16,17).

Jesus is the only way to be saved. You can come to Him as you are. Don't worry about getting your life right first, that's His job. His arms are wide open and He won't push you away. When you mess up, as we all do, repent and He'll forgive you. He'll wash away your sin and won't remember it anymore. Imagine a life without guilt and shame, where you don't have to carry it anymore because He carried it to the cross for you!

He'll never leave you. When He says, "I am with you always, even to the end" (Matt. 28:20),

He means it. His Spirit will be with you wherever you go.

"Where can I go from Your Spirit? Or where can I flee from Your presence? If I ascend into heaven, You are there; If I make my bed in hell, behold, You are there. If I take the wings of the morning, And dwell in the uttermost parts of the sea, Even there Your hand shall lead me, And Your right hand shall hold me" (Ps. 139:7–10).

If you would, close your eyes and imagine with me. You're in your cell. Jesus walks in. He holds out His hand to you. He breathes your name and says, "Follow Me" (John 8:12).

If you desire the everlasting life He offers you, then receive His gift of eternal life (Rom. 6:23). If you reject it, you will be separated from Him forever and your name will not be found in the Book of Life (Rev. 20:12–15).

His Word says, "If you confess with your mouth the Lord Jesus and believe in your heart that God has raised Him from the dead, you will be saved" (Rom. 10:9).

Chapter 12

NEW DAY

Therefore, if anyone is in Christ, he is a new creation; old things have passed away; behold, all things have become new.
~2 Corinthians 5:17

It's a new day. You have a brand-new life with a fresh start in the Lord. Get to know the One who loves you most. "And this is eternal life, that they may know You, the only true God, and Jesus Christ whom You have sent" (John 17:3). Talk with Him and listen quietly to Him every day. Trust Him with all your heart, because He will never fail you.

His word is a lamp for your feet and light for your path. Ask Him for the word that illuminates your path and the grace to walk it because it's impossible in your own strength. Lean on Him and His Holy Spirit will empower you. "I can do all things through Christ who strengthens me" (Phil. 4:13).

As you walk with God, keep in mind that life as a believer will not be perfect, but it will be good. When challenges come, don't give up, because He hasn't given up on you. Squeeze your right hand. He's holding it, saying to you, "Fear not, I will help you" (Isa. 41:13). The God of all creation is for you, and He can work all things out in ways you haven't thought of. Wait on Him; even your pain won't be wasted.

The Word says, "'God resists the proud, But gives grace to the humble.' Therefore humble yourselves under the mighty hand of God, that He may exalt you in due time, casting all your care upon Him, for He cares for you. Be sober, be vigilant; because your adversary the devil walks about like a roaring lion, seeking whom he may devour" (1 Pet. 5:5–8).

God knows the pain is too great for you. Throw your cares on Him and He will comfort you. He is the God of all comfort (2 Cor. 1:3). Be sober and alert. The devil wants you in bondage to addiction because he's the thief that comes to steal, kill, and destroy. Don't let him.

"For we do not wrestle against flesh and blood, but against principalities, against powers, against the rulers of the darkness of this age, against spiritual hosts of wickedness in the heavenly places" (Eph. 6:12).

The enemy is fierce, but he's nothing compared to God. You can submit to God, resist the devil, and he will flee from you (James 4:7). As a believer, you don't need to fear him because God gives you authority over him (Luke 10:19). Instead, fear God.

He says to you, "The past is not your God, I am. Trust Me with the desires of your heart and see what I will do with them. Follow Jesus. He is the way, the truth, and the life. I love you. I always have and I always will."

As I write, correctional facilities are closed to visitors and volunteers because of a pandemic. But when they're open, I visit my son regularly. I'm getting to know him better than I did before. He shares his life with me, a privilege I don't take for granted. We sharpen each other as iron sharpens iron. He encourages me to press on and stay motivated. He is a blessing to me. I love him.

I volunteered at the jail for six years, meeting wonderful people. We grew together as we worshiped the Lord and ministered to each other. It was an honor to be a part of their journey. I look forward to more opportunities to serve and to see the incarcerated grow in the love of Jesus and the truth of who they are in Him.

I know a Christian pastor who helped regularly in prison. He ministered on three-and-a-half-day retreats, where they would serve cookies. He needed cookies. Dozens of fresh cookies with the best ingredients.

Yeah, I baked them some cookies.

May the LORD answer you in the day of trouble;
May the name of the God of Jacob defend you;
May He send you help from the sanctuary,
And strengthen you out of Zion;
May He remember all your offerings,
And accept your burnt sacrifice. *Selah*
May He grant you according to your heart's desire,
And fulfill all your purpose.
We will rejoice in your salvation,
And in the name of our God we will set up our banners!
May the LORD fulfill all your petitions.
Now I know that the LORD saves His anointed;
He will answer him from His holy heaven
With the saving strength of His right hand.
Some trust in chariots, and some in horses;

But we will remember the name of the LORD
our God.
They have bowed down and fallen;
But we have risen and stand upright.
Save, LORD!
May the King answer us when we call. (Psalm 20)

"Therefore, my beloved and longed-for breth-
ren, my joy and crown, so stand fast in the Lord,
beloved" (Phil. 4:1).

Bibliography

1. Epps, Keith. "Idlewild Man Jailed in Stabbing Death." *The Freelance Star* (Fredericksburg, VA), October 13, 2011.

2. Kent, Carol. *Between a Rock and a Grace Place: Divine Surprises in the Tight Spots of Life*. Michigan: Zondervan, 2010.

3. Ratcliff, Roy, with Lindy Adams. *Dark Journey Deep Grace: Jeffrey Dahmer's Story of Faith*. Texas: Leafwood Publishers, 2006.

YOUR THOUGHTS

YOUR THOUGHTS

_____

_____

_____

_____

_____

_____

_____

_____

_____

_____

_____

_____

_____

_____

_____

_____

_____

_____

_____

_____

_____

_____

_____

_____

_____

YOUR THOUGHTS

YOUR THOUGHTS

YOUR THOUGHTS

_____
_____
_____
_____
_____
_____
_____
_____
_____
_____
_____
_____
_____
_____
_____
_____
_____
_____
_____
_____
_____
_____
_____
_____

YOUR THOUGHTS

YOUR THOUGHTS

YOUR THOUGHTS

YOUR THOUGHTS

Your Thoughts

YOUR THOUGHTS

YOUR THOUGHTS

CPSIA information can be obtained
at www.ICGtesting.com
Printed in the USA
BVHW031237260722
643033BV00014B/994